no
matter
how
it
ends
a
bluebird's
song

Kat Lehmann

Rattle | *Studio City, California* | 2025

Layout and design by Timothy Green

Cover art by Rachel Bingaman
"Spring Breathes," 2022
Oil on canvas

ISBN: 978-1-931307-60-4

First edition

Rattle Foundation
12411 Ventura Blvd
Studio City, CA 91604
www.rattle.com

Contents

no
matter
how
it
ends
a
bluebird's
song

1: *trail.*

two
   days
after
   the
first
   dose
the
   world
falls
   into
starlings

the whale in my limbs stranded mid-trail

where the trees are my before picture

wondering what
the flying flock …
overhead crows

what could have been a chestful of hUmMiNgBiRdS

suddenly fishless my ocean pinned under the atmosphere

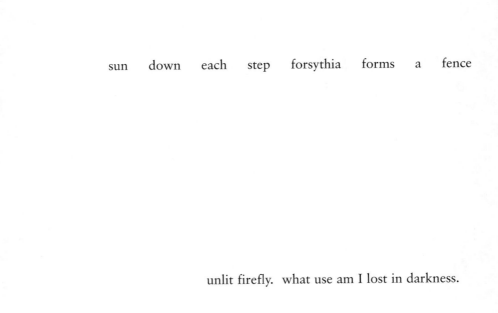

sun   down   each   step   forsythia   forms   a   fence

unlit firefly. what use am I lost in darkness.

how to make it home again on earth as it is in

2: *room.*

the doctor shrugs nothing he can   for me withering wind

antarctica brain without fog penguins

(deleting the dictionary the mountain stream comes and goes) moonlighting

the cats
change shifts

ghost orchid
a sense of psyche
absent

w a n i n g
gibbous
forgett
ing
to
e
a
t

sink
ing
in
to
my
self
the
occ a s i o n a l
                you

trapped in a body the star a sky wanders

who am I without my mind dandelion

3: *fatigue.*

fir
st fern f
ading
into
the pri
mal

sunset window the tree becomes my face

beyond the bed
a lilt of voices live
my former life

seagull prints
the party held
without me

                              gathering dark
                              telling the children
                              I can't

            sudden
                      rain
              their
giggles
                  slip
          through
my
          hands

fatigue days
everything to do
with *et cetera*

outside the window frames a Rothko a raven

becoming the bed be still and know

4: clinic.

clinic exam
the one-fits-all
of paper pants

ICD
codes
the
taxonomy
of
raptors

still inside a cricket the magnet measures my viscera

blood letting each use and disclosure

blue
butterfly
needle
tip
of
the
scar
on
this
rem
ain
ing
ve
in
.

torn vein
I make a Pollock
of the sheets

pulse oximeter
the data but also
the hypothesis

river cloud
the X of this body
unsolvable

left less than a cloudless sulfur adrift in an illness

5: shadowwwww.

first diagnosis
I follow the rabbit
down a familiar hole

berry thorns
what doesn't fit
the paradigm

medical exemption
a committee of strangers
votes on my life

anonymous my shadow follows into the autumn meadow

sleepless the ceiling fan pushes the dark around

long night
a life without me

```
              a
            pine
           tree I
         stand all
         day in my
        shadowwwww
```

departing geese
the day and time
not of my knowing

       writing our will only two things matter

6: *reaching.*

snowstorm
the bed piled heavy
with cats

an ark built for one winter rain

killing frost to die only once

Venn raindrops winter circles into one

caught in four chambers the nautilus core of a prayer

still waters from the shadows I shall not want

reaching
toward
the
spring
sea
bottom
promises
to
myself

is it ok to hope an ocean road

no matter how it ends a bluebird's song

7: *shake.*

gyroscope my vertigo slows from van Gogh to blue skies

slow rowing in the basement lake one minute   two more   three

false spring
the lightening and lengthening
of symptoms

word finding all the birds are chickadees

born a tree how easy the river speaks

as much as I want to be still these wild flowers

morning sea
I shake the night
from my wings

second
   dose
forsythia
   with
  a
   chance
     of
rain

         fear
       my
      me
    beco
    un
    I
    us
    croc
    w
    sno

8: returns.

moon my mind
moon by moon my mind pines
moon by moon my mind through the pines
moon by moon my mind returns through the pines

what is left of the light no longer scatters

brown leaf carpet
I learn to walk
on what came before

first sun
the tears of not
ending

two years gone barefoot in the garden

sun warmed tomatoes and my bones ripe

finding myself
where I least expect
puddle moon

giving birth to healing what to name it

sea-smoothed stone
the part of me
still here

9: *here.*

spring hike
how close I came
to deering

after winter rains the river spoken here

deep green
the oxygen trail
all adjectives

so much to talk about tiger lilies

filling my cup
all the octaves
in a river

peony opening my heart too close to the surface

among the views
of blues and greens
a tree cathedral

but what if it all works out cherry blossoms

an answer without end quotes the forest stream

Acknowledgments

Deep gratitude to my family and friends who have supported me in countless ways, even when they did not know the full story at the time. Special thanks to *Rattle* for including contemporary haiku in the literary conversation. My humble appreciation to the editors of the below venues in which the original versions of the following poems first appeared:

AHA Haiku Contest: "snowstorm the bed"

Akitsu Quarterly: "so much to talk about"

ant ant ant ant ant: "giving birth to healing"

Bones: "antarctica brain" and "Venn raindrops"

#FemkuMag: "first diagnosis I follow"

Frogpond: "where the trees are," "seagull prints," and "an answer without end quotes"

Haiku International Association Haiku Contest: "sea-smoothed stone"

Ito En Art of Haiku Contest: "sudden rain their giggles," "filling my cup," "sleepless the ceiling fan," and "no matter how it ends"

Kingfisher: "morning sea," "trapped in a body," and "peony opening my heart"

Modern Haiku: "anonymous my shadow" and "snow crocus I unbecome"

Neighborhood Haiku Contest, Lexington, Massachusetts Council for the Arts: "finding myself"

A New Resonance: Emerging Voices in English-Language Haiku (Red Moon Press, 2023): "suddenly fishless," "is it ok to hope," "born a tree," and "what is left of the light"

Pan Haiku Reader: "two days after" and "long night a life"

Password: "outside the window frames" and "first fern fading"

Sonic Boom: "fatigue days"

Under the Basho: "sunset window," "sun warmed tomatoes," and "still inside a cricket"

Vancouver Cherry Blossom Festival Haiku Invitational: "but what if"

Wales Haiku Journal: "brown leaf carpet"

ABOUT THE RATTLE CHAPBOOK SERIES

The Rattle Chapbook Series publishes and distributes a chapbook to all of *Rattle*'s print subscribers along with each quarterly issue of the magazine. Most selections are made through the annual Rattle Chapbook Prize competition (deadline: January 15ᵗʰ). For more information, and to order other chapbooks from the series, visit our website.

www.Rattle.com/chapbooks